Night of the Dolls

A FANTASY DRAMA IN ONE ACT BY
F. E. M. AGNEW

Acting time 25 minutes, approximately.

822.91

E N G L I S H   T H E A T R E   G U I L D
Ascot House, 52 Dean Street,
London, W.1.

CHARACTERS

JANE—A young reporter.

MISS WITCHERLY—A scientist with a passion for collecting dolls.

DOLLS:

EGYPT—An Egyptian grave doll.

BETTY—A Witch doll, used for spell-binding in the 15th century.

MIMI—A French dress-modelling doll (late 1840's).

DUTCH—A wooden Dutch doll, made by Miss Witcherly.

MOD—A replica of a modern "Beat Group" Singer. Made by Miss Witcherly.

NIGHT OF THE DOLLS

SCENE:—A room with a table on which are some half made garments and a sewing machine. Along a side wall is a chemistry bench, with bottles and glass retorts. One or two chairs. At the back is a curtained off area, behind which stand the life-sized dolls in boxes (which should be replicas of doll boxes.)

(*Note: The curtain should be divided so that one doll at a time may be shown.*)

As the scene opens MISS WITCHERLY *is being interviewed by* JANE, *a young reporter.*

JANE. It is very good of you to see me, Miss Witcherly, and I am thrilled to think that I am to be allowed to report on your hobby.

MISS WITCHERLY. Not at all.

JANE. I am told that your collection of dressed dolls is absolutely fabulous.

MISS WITCHERLY. I would say quite unique. I have devoted a number of years to my "hobby", as you call it, and I have never granted an interview before. But this time it is different. We have mutual friends, you see.

JANE. Oh, have we?

MISS WITCHERLY. My colleague at the laboratory— Dr. Mitchell.

JANE. Really? (*She looks embarrassed.*)

MISS WITCHERLY. Yes, didn't you know?

JANE. No, I didn't. Now, Miss Witcherly, I shall be terribly grateful for all the information you can give me about the dolls. My Editor is keenly interested.

MISS WITCHERLY. All the information? That would take too long I fear. But you are wondering where I keep my dolls. The smaller ones are in the next room— we will come to them presently. I have the jewels of my collection—the rare and the unusual—in here.

JANE. How exciting! (*She looks round room, then opens her note book.*)

MISS WITCHERLY. The more I have delved into the history of dolls the more fascinating it has become . . . . and the more eerie.

JANE. Eerie, Miss Witcherly? Dolls are only toys after all.

MISS WITCHERLY. Each thing created—whether by man or the supernatural—draws some power, or shall we call it life force, to itself. Don't you agree, Miss . . . . . ?

JANE. Oh, please call me Jane. Everyone does. But do go on about your dolls.

MISS WITCHERLY. Yes—er—the dolls. I keep my life sized dolls in here.

JANE. Life size? They are hardly dolls then, are they? More a Madame Tussaud effort.

MISS WITCHERLY. No, no, no! You don't get the point, Jane. Her wax figures are copies of human beings. My dolls are dolls. Life size dolls were not so unusual in earlier days. No, indeed.

JANE. I can't wait to see them.

MISS WITCHERLY. Well, then!

(*She goes back stage and draws aside curtain so as to show the Egyptian doll, which is standing perfectly rigid in her box. She is dressed in wrappings of chrome yellow, brown and turquoise. Her face is a yellowish brown, with numerous black crack lines traced on it.* JANE *recoils*).

Don't you like the look of her Jane? She is a very good specimen. She was fated to be entombed to amuse the corpse of an Egyptian princess in the world of shades. (*She laughs, shrilly*). I rescued her, but she has to be satisfied with rather more lowly company here. Don't you, Egypt?

JANE. Hush!

MISS WITCHERLY. Ah! So you begin to feel it. Created things do gather an aura around themselves don't they?

JANE. But, Miss Witcherly, how *could* she have survived all these years. Surely, she would have crumbled to dust.

MISS WITCHERLY. Aha! I thought you would ask that question. Of course she would not have survived once she came in contact with the air; but I have some skill with preserving fluids—and where it crumbled I renewed the fabric very carefully. I suppose there is not much of the original left, actually, and yet so gradual have been the substitutions, I feel the essence of her personality is still contained in that figure you see before you. After all, we humans are entirely renewed physically within the span of seven years—or so we were told when we were children—yet we retain the same characteristics and nature.

JANE. There is something daunting about her.

MISS WITCHERLY. My next doll won't make you feel nervous.

JANE. I'm not nervous.

MISS WITCHERLY. No? Perhaps you should be. (*She draws curtain over* EGYPT). You know that some Eastern religions do not permit human likenesses to be painted or modelled. Could it be that they sense the power lying dormant in graven images? Ah, well. (*She draws the next curtain, exposing a delightfully dressed doll, clothed in the French style of the late* 1840's.)

JANE. How delightful!

MISS WITCHERLY. Yes, isn't she? But she is vain, aren't you, Mimi? Just see the expression in her eyes. This young lady has an interesting history and I was fortunate to get her.

JANE (*scribbling in note-book*). Yes?

MISS WITCHERLY. Queen Victoria, with her daughter the Princess Royal, who was then a young girl, was invited to the French Court on a visit. Before their departure from England the Emperor tactfully despatched this doll to the princess, fully dressed in the latest style, in order to show the child's mother how the princess should be fitted out for such an occasion. Royal taste in dress at that period was, shall we say, somewhat inartistic . . . . as I expect you will know—all tartan or tulle—and in this way Napoleon could guide his Royal visitors without giving offence. Very tactful, was it not?

JANE (*scribbling busily*). My women readers will love this. What beautiful hand-work on that dress—and what style! I can't get used to the dolls being so *large*!

MISS WITCHERLY. Life-sized, Jane, as I said before. Not unusual in days gone by. I find them quite companionable. They never change though love and friends grow cold.

JANE. This is so much more interesting than I had imagined . . . . but, Miss Witcherly, how does it tie in with your work—your scientific research, I mean? Anything to do with chemistry seems rather masculine to the lay man; but let's face it, dolls are completely and utterly feminine.

MISS WITCHERLY. Come, Jane, you as a journalist must have found out that no woman is completely feminine, nor any man completely masculine. Now for my piece-de-resistance. (*She shuts curtain over* MIMI *and open next curtain, to disclose a horrible looking effigy, with tousled hair and a wax face which has partially melted. It is dressed in dark grey tattered sixteenth century clothes, while over the heart is a rusty stain. The limbs are sprawled like those of a rag doll which has been thrown down. (Note: A mask is suggested for this character.)*

JANE (*recoiling*). It's horrible! Horrible! What is it?

MISS WITCHERLY. She's quite harmless, I assure you—unless we have a witch in the vicinity. (*She gives her hysterical, uncharacteristic laugh again.*)

JANE. But what is it? Oh, do cover it up.

MISS WITCHERLY. Poor Betty. The lady doesn't like you. (*She straightens the dolls arms and head*). There! That's better. I must tell you Jane that she was found after old Peg Humphrey, a witch if ever there was one, was burned. In the reign of Henry the Eighth it was.

JANE. So that is a witch doll.

MISS WITCHERLY. Yes, yes. There are many kinds. Old Peg obviously bore someone a grudge, or was well paid to induce her to fashion so large a doll on which to work her spells. I wonder how long it took?

JANE. To make it?

MISS WITCHERLY. No, no. To kill the victim—for kill him it did.

JANE. That is ridiculous. Things like that just don't happen.

MISS WITCHERLY. No? Give me your hand. (*She takes Jane's hand and presses it to the stain over the doll's heart.*) There!

JANE (*looks at her hand and rubs it convulsively*). Ugh! It's damp! My hand is stained!

MISS WITCHERLY. She still bleeds.

JANE. It's a trick!

MISS WITCHERLY. I do not play tricks. You asked to see and I am showing you. If you care to look in any Reference Library you will find that this is a well known manifestation. (*She looks closely again at the doll*). H'mm I'm afraid Betty is one of my less successful preservations. It could be the dampness—the blood, perhaps.

JANE. Blood! I don't think I can include that in my article. People now-a-days just wouldn't believe it . . . . well . . . . would they? It's so fantastic — so—

MISS WITCHERLY. What about you, Jane. Having seen, do you believe?

JANE. I - I - I don't *want* to!

MISS WITCHERLY. Our good King Hal did. He took witches quite seriously, and he was an intelligent man, though I have never cared for his morals. He might have been a Hollywood star—his collection of wives would hardly have been noticed there. Don't you agree, Jane?

JANE. He lived so long ago—I have hardly thought about him.

MISS WITCHERLY. Have you not? You should, you know. You are young and attractive and are sure to marry. Take my advice and choose a faithful type. Not a Doctor Mitchell.

JANE. Really, Miss Witcherly, you mustn't speak in that way about my friend.

MISS WITCHERLY. He is my friend, too—but it doesn't blind me as to his nature. Why! You look quite upset? Are you sure he is just a friend to you?

JANE. It's nothing to do with you.

MISS WITCHERLY (*very coldly*). No, of course not. Good night, Miss eh- Jane. (*There is a long pause while* JANE, *who badly wants to complete the interview, regains her temper.*)

JANE. Oh, dear. Look, I'm sorry I lost my temper . . . . but . . . . Malcolm—Dr Mitchell and I are engaged, though we haven't announced it yet, so you see . . . .

MISS WITCHERLY (*very quietly*). Yes, I see. Now that *is* interesting. You must let me be the first—the very first to wish you happiness. And don't worry—I daresay he will be different now.

JANE. Different?

MISS WITCHERLY. Don't *worry*! Let us get on with this doll feature, shall we? You asked me how my scientific training fitted in with my collector's hobby. It does—wonderfully well. See this. (*She goes to a box and takes out a small fur covered toy dog.*)

JANE (*taking the dog from her*). O-h-h! This is something!

MISS WITCHERLY. You think so? You really like it?

JANE. Oh, yes. It is perfect in every detail.

MISS WITCHERLY. Yes, it is. Quite perfect. In every detail.

JANE. Did you make it?

MISS WITCHERLY. In a sense.

JANE. How do you mean?

MISS WITCHERLY. Poor, small animal. He was killed —poisoned—just about the time I had perfected the process I have been working on for so long, and so I tried the drug on the remains. And it works! It really works! Three months and not one sign of deterioration. No signs at all! You see what this could mean?

JANE. A real dog! It's terribly clever of you. (*She hastily thrusts the dog back into Miss Witcherly's hands*). But I don't like it! It is wrong—unnatural!

MISS WITCHERLY. You must keep an open mind, my young friend. Knowledge is never wasted.

JANE. But what possible use can this be? Dead creatures should be left in peace, till they blend again into the earth from which they came. Oh, dear, I'm sounding quite biblical.

MISS WITCHERLY. But think of the comfort my discovery could give. A pet who dies could now be preserved indefinitely, and fondled by its owner. There is no reason why it should not be successful with human beings, though I haven't been able to try that, yet. Suppose, just for a moment, that you were to pass on—as the American Garden of Rest promoters so euphemistically cloak the stark fact of death—how comforting for your Malcolm to be able to enshrine you in his bachelor flat—or vice versa, should he " pass on " first. (*She laughs.*)

JANE. Don't!

MISS WITCHERLY. I'm sorry. Just a whimsy. We scientists are apt to become a little hard, I fear. Now what do you want to do next?

JANE. I would like to take some photos if you would allow me.

MISS WITCHERLY. Certainly—but no pictures of my little dog. We are not going to talk about you yet—are we, my poppet? (*She strokes and coos at the dog.*)

JANE. I shall have to use a flash—it's rather dark in here. Oh, lord, I've left my camera behind. If I dash off for it I can be back in a few minutes.

MISS WITCHERLY. Before you go there are two more life sized dolls I must show you. (*She opens curtains to show* DUTCH DOLL *and* MOD DOLL.) These I made entirely with my own hands.

JANE. They are marvellous. I adore the wooden doll. Do you know, my grandmother still has one that was given her when she was a little girl. Not so large as this one, of course. What do you call the other one?

MISS WITCHERLY. "MOD" Typical of today.

JANE. Of course! She is fabulous—absolutely and completely mod. (MISS WITCHERLY *pulls curtain and*

MISS WITCHERLY *and* JANE *exit.)*

(There is a short silence and then the curtains cover-
ing the dolls are jerkily opened. EGYPT, MIMI *and*
BETTY *step out stiffly.* MOD *and* DUTCH *are still*
immobile. The three dolls drape themselves around
the room as though quite at home in it. They sit or
stand in grotesque " doll " attitudes.)

EGYPT. How stiff my limbs have become. These cold
English nights. I long to be lovingly massaged with
unguents from Memphis.

BETTY (*eagerly*). I'll rub 'ee. As I used to rub She.
Made the salve with 'er own 'ands, did old Peg.

EGYPT. Your salves—they are unholy! Have I not
said cow-dung as a medicament is unclean, unthinkable!

BETTY. Unclean! 'Oo be you to talk of "unclean?"
Wot about your first dwelling-place? The grave b'aint
none too clean; or so I've allers 'eard tell.

MIMI. 'Ow 'orrible! Such vulgaire thoughts always
you express. You and I, Egypt, at least are familiar wiz
the Royal Courts—I of la belle France, and you of ze
pagan Nile. You should be-ave bettaire.

EGYPT. Do not try to persuade me that the Court of
France was pure and lofty, Mimi, for my ancient wisdom
tells me differently.

MIMI. Pouf! 'Ow could you know anyzing—entombed
for centuries. But I, Mimi, tell you that at ze Court of
France we do not marry our brothers, at least, as was ze
'abit of your Royalty.

EGYPT (*shrugging*). Better had they done so. The
kings and queens of Egypt were thoroughbred; but the
common people executed your plebeian Royalty.

MOD DOLL (*emerging from behind curtain, yawning*).
Oh, Gawd, I kipped too long. Why couldn't yah wake
us? Come out, Dutch. What's cooking.

(DUTCH *walks out stiffly to join* MOD.)

BETTY. *She's* brewing a Hell broth. That's what be
cooking.

DUTCH. Ya?

MOD. Coo! Wadd'ya mean? Give!

MIMI. Betty—Egypt—wait! Do not trust 'er. (*Points to* MOD.) She is a poor, new thing. Not as we are.

MOD. New? Wot's wrong with bein' new? I'm fab, that's wot I am—Fab!

EGYPT. Explain, Mimi.

MIMI. You do not compre'end? The Witcherly woman *made* her. She is the thing of 'er 'ands, and may be—

BETTY. A creature of the woman. That'd be proper comical.

EGYPT. Mod doll, I will put you in a trance, and make you speak truth. (*She approaches* MOD *threateningly*).

MOD. Don't *trouble*. Can't stand the old trout's guts, meself. (MIMI *squeaks in horror*). She's rotten to the core, that one.

DUTCH. Yah! Also me she made, but her I hate.

BETTY. Ay! That sweet little dog—t'was she who gave him the poisoned potion.

EGYPT. Wanton destruction! Had she intended to lay him at his mistress's feet in the dark tomb, it would have been understandable.

MOD. Carnt yer keep orf bone-yards, Egypt? It's like 'aving a cat walk over yer grave. Any'ow, wot's the old trout up to?

EGYPT. She means to harm the Jane girl.

MIMI. Vraiment! I, too, think it.

DUTCH. But vy?

EGYPT. Did you not hearken? The Professor, who the Witcherly woman wished to take for her paramour, has chosen the Jane—and moreover, has asked her hand in marriage.

MOD (*screams with laughter*). Coo! "Take for 'er paramour!" I'll say—wiv nobs on! D'ya remember the night she brought 'im up 'ere—showed 'im all 'er dolls an' bits er chemistry—then poured 'im a whacking great snifter an' tried ter git matey. But 'ee wasn' 'avin' none.

DUTCH. Love! Passion! Vot is it but a sickness—a fever of the mind.

MOD. Dunno about that—we ain't all got your wooden 'eaded what-yer-may-call-it—but as I said, 'ee wasn't 'avin' none.

BETTY. Old Peg, my mistress, would ha' made 'ee a love potion. She were a good mistress — no better witch than she in the West country. I'd put my hand to it. But she burned for all that.

MIMI. Allow us to forget your unsavoury origins, I beg.

BETTY. Never mind my er- what you said. If t'werent for the bits of magic I've picked up from Old Peg, it's stuck in those boxes till the last Trump you'd be. No midnight cavortings for you, my fine lady. But now 'tis the young Jane I be thinking on. In proper peril she be. I feel it in my bloody wound: it throbs a warning. There is witch-craft—black witch-craft in the air.

MOD. Yer don't say. It might be good fer a giggle, like. Wot are we goin' ter do?

EGYPT. Do? Is it our concern should harm come to her? She is very *young*, not only in years but intellectually. Many there are of her undistinguished breed. She is of no great value.

MIMI. Come, Egypt!

EGYPT. Did you hear her philosophising? So naive the sacred cats would have smiled had they heard her.

BETTY. But are we to let *her* work her evil will?

MIMI. I like this girl—and she has an appreciation of haute couture—mais enfin, we 'ave not much to lighten our ennui in this so drab room. It could be très amusant to watch what ze witch will do to 'er.

MOD. Dunno—can't say I dig that; though I'd see most anything fer a giggle, like.

DUTCH. Dig it? Vot iss " dig it "?

MOD. Skip it—yer wouldn't unnerstand.

EGYPT. The maid returns soon, and *she* is waiting.

MIMI. Is it zat your eyes see through walls, Egypt?

EGYPT. Listen! She is below making music on the zither. (*They listen*).

MOD. Ha-ha-ha—ya mean 'er transistor. She's switched it orf nah. We'd better nip back to our pre-fabs.

EGYPT. The maiden's fate will be decided in this room.

BETTY. On a night such as this, with the moon at the full and black clouds racing across the face of it, fates may be changed by spells and incantations.

MIMI. 'Ow disagreeable!

BETTY. Mayhap my words be unpleasing, but it is me, Betty, who minded enough of old Peg's arts to give you all freedom after sunset, when bats squeak and fly widder-shins—and *Her* knowing naught of it, he-he-he.

EGYPT (*clasping her forehead*). Faint memories stir in me—they come and go like a wanton breeze—memories of such spirit power—but yet the key eludes me. Some day, some night I shall remember, and then *your* feeble spells will shiver into nothingness.

BETTY. Well, 'ee aven't minded yet. But take heed—should we leave our boxes again this night t'will be the end to our freedom. 'Tis as much as I can do ter give 'ee life fer a little—so take heed—my spells b'aint so strong as my mistress's.

MOD. Do turn it up, mate. Cavey!

(*The dolls get back into their boxes and draw the curtains. The door opens and* MISS WITCHERLY *comes in. She now wears black overalls and her hair is hidden under a black skull cap. She has a strange expression on her face. She carries a tray with two wine-glasses, a bottle of wine and a phial of tablets. She puts some tablets into one of the glasses, then fills both with wine. She then takes out a syringe, fills it then hides it under a cloth. She picks up the small dog, fondles it and puts it down again. Hearing a sound, she hurries out.)*

          Exit MISS WITCHERLY.

(The Dolls look through curtains).

DUTCH. She downstairs has gone, the girl to let in.

MOD. Look out! She's comin' upstairs.

(The curtains are drawn and there is a slight pause before JANE *enters.)*

JANE (*opening curtain of* MIMI'S *box*). How graceful you are—and what elegant clothes. You might almost be alive—I wish you were alive; it's rather frightening in here. And I'm sure you would be fun to talk with   What tales you could tell of the little Princess and her visit to the Emperor of France. (*She pulls back the curtain which covers* EGYPT.) To you I would come for advice, O Egypt. You look so wise and dignified I would trust you . . . even with my life. (*She uncovers* DUTCH). Your smooth hair and apple cheeks bring back memories. When I was a little girl I played with a doll like you, in my grandmother's house, and I loved her for her honesty and her strong wooden frame. (*Uncovers* MOD.) Now, I'm a bit wary of real girls like you—but I feel we might be friends. Oh, you may smile and pretend you care for nothing, but I think that you do. Oh, dear, I'm talking as though you were alive. (*Uncovers* BETTY.) I would be *very polite to you*—but you might be the most interesting of all. Such tales of Courtly love and tragic executions— of sunlit days filled with the music of lute and harp . . . . and dark, wild nights when witches' coverns shrieked and whirled on the windswept moors, and desperate ladies slipped love potions into goblets of red wine. (*Here* BETTY *lurches sideways and with a nervous cry* JANE *pulls the curtains to.*)

          (*Enter* MISS WITCHERLY.)

JANE. O, I haven't begun yet, I'm afraid.

MISS WITCHERLY. Never mind. Have some sherry.

JANE. No—no thank you Miss Witcherly. I must'nt be too long.

MISS WITCHERLY. Is Dr. Mitchell waiting? Come, Jane, it will do you good. You look rather pale. (*She proffers the glass which has been doctored.*)

JANE. Well . . . . thank you. (*She drinks*). Now, I'd better get down to it.

MISS WITCHERLY. No hurry. Finish your sherry first. Don't you like it?

JANE. It's rather dry—but the effect will be the same, won't it?

MISS WITCHERLY. You young people always rush so.

JANE (*drinking*). Do we? I suppose we do; but it doesn't feel like rushing. I think that everyone has their own natural pace—like the cruising speed of a car—and it is awfully important to be understanding about it.

MISS WITCHERLY. Tell me more.

JANE. Well . . . . the quick people are impatient of the slow, and the slow get flustered by—and dislike— the quickness of the quick. If only they would leave each other to go as they please . . . . (*She yawns.*) That was strong sherry . . . . and you mustn't encourage me to talk nonsense.

MISS WITCHERLY. Let me fill your glass.

JANE (*laughing a little tipsily*). No *thank* you—I should be taking op, art pictures, and my editor wouldn't like that—he wouldn't like it at all.

MISS WITCHERLY. Very well—perhaps you had better take your photographs. It wouldn't do to keep Dr. Mitchell waiting, would it?

JANE. Oh, he won't mind.

MISS WITCHERLY. No? (JANE *tries to rise, but cannot.*) What are you waiting for, Jane?

JANE. I - I feel very odd.

MISS WITCHERLY (*laughing*). Oh, come! Or was it only sherry?

JANE. Wh-what?

MISS WITCHERLY. I didn't think it would act so quickly . . . . interesting.

JANE. What are you saying?

MISS WITCHERLY. Very interesting.

JANE. You - you put something in it. Why?

MISS WITCHERLY. Don't be so silly. Stand up! (JANE *tries to rise, but is helpless.*)

JANE. I - I can't. What have you done?

MISS WITCHERLY. I? I'll tell you. I have just put a strong sleeping draught in your drink.

JANE. Why?

MISS WITCHERLY. There is nothing for you to worry about. You won't feel anything.

JANE. *Feel* anything? You look so strange, you frighten me. Oh, please don't—don't—

MISS WITCHERLY. Stop trying to plead with me, you doll-faced little fool. What can he see in you—youth, I suppose. Well, he shall have you, in the full bloom of youth—have you for ever. For you will never grow any older, Jane.

JANE. Oh, you're mad! (*She again struggles to get up, but cannot.*)

(MISS WITCHERLY *has picked up the telephone and is dialling a number.*)

MISS WITCHERLY. Oh, no—I am doing you both a kindness. Because I love him, do you hear? Love him with a passion you could not begin to understand. So, I will stop the clock—he shall have you as you are tonight.

You will never nag, or argue, Jane, or bore him with your mediocre remarks—nor will you grow faded or fat. Because you are to be turned into a doll . . . a big, beautiful doll. (JANE *screams thinly.* MISS WITCHERLY *has now obtained the telephone number*). Oh, is that Malcolm Mitchell? This is Sabine Witcherly. Your Jane is feeling rather unwell. Yes. I think you should come and fetch her. I think she would like to speak to you. (*She puts telephone to* JANE'S *lips.*)

JANE. Oh . . . darling . . . help me, help . . . She's mad . . . (*She screams again as* MISS WITCHERLY *picks up the syringe.*) Keep away . . . Ah-h-h! (*She collapses, unconscious.*)

MISS WITCHERLY. I must hang up now, dear colleague. Don't be long. I'm sure you will find my experiment most interesting. I'm going to give her an injection which should preserve her . . . . No, I said preserve. (*She laughs.*) Good-bye. Hurry! Though it doesn't matter whether you do or no, really. You will have all the time in the world. What? The police? Oh, they won't believe you. She will *be* a doll you see. One of my collection. But I shall give her to *you.* (*She laughs and puts down receiver. Then she turns to the unconscious Jane, pushes up her sleeve and fiddles with the syringe. There is a slight sound and she turns, to see the curtains swept back and the dolls approach, stiffly and menacingly. She is paralysed with fear.*)

MISS WITCHERLY. Go back—go back!

(EGYPT *takes the syringe from her nerveless hand while* MOD *and* DUTCH *hold her arms, and old* BETTY *hovers, eagerly.* MIMI *stands apart, twisting her curls, and looking on with cool amusement.* EGYPT *lifts the syringe as though about to perform a ritual,* MIMI *comes near to* MISS WITCHERLY, *so that she is hidden from the audience. There is a scream, a pause, and* MISS WITCHERLY *stiffens and becomes lifeless.*)

BETTY. Well, me dears, 'tis the end for we—but t'was worth it, he-he-he!

(*One by one the dolls subside, like toys thrown down by a child, and while* JANE, *unharmed, lies uncon- scious, footsteps are heard on the stairs, and a man's voice calling* "Jane! Jane! I'm coming. I'm coming, my darling. Jane!").

CURTAIN.

Other all-woman One Act Plays by F. E. M. Agnew include:—

PROPERTIES

Laboratory table.
Shelves.
Bottles, etc.
Telephone,
Telephone table,
3 chairs.
Sewing table.
Low drinks table.
Curtains.
5 Doll boxes.
Toy dog (fur). Basket.
Carpet.
Lamps.

PERSONAL PROPERTIES

MISS WITCHERLY: Cigarettes.
Tray with drinks
Tablets.
Syringe.
Liquid for Syringe.

JANE: Note book and pencil.
Handbag.
(2nd entrance) Camera.

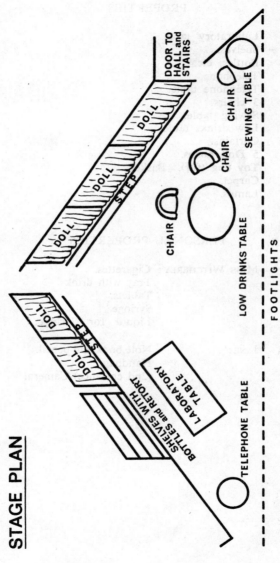